Cartoon Story Starters

Grades 4-6

Written by Tom Goldsmith
Illustrated by Tom Goldsmith

About the author:
Tom Goldsmith is an accomplished cartoonist whose work can be regularly seen in a number of magazines, books, and periodicals through out North America. A member of the National Cartoonists Society, Tom is passionate about cartooning and teaching children to express themselves and their sense of humor. Learn more at www.Timberdoodles.com.

ISBN 978-1-55035-904-6
Copyright 2007
All Rights Reserved * Printed in Canada

Published in the United States by:
On The Mark Press
3909 Witmer Road PMB 175
Niagara Falls, New York
14305
www.onthemarkpress.com

Published in Canada by:
S&S Learning Materials
15 Dairy Avenue
Napanee, Ontario
K7R 1M4
www.sslearning.com

At  Glance

Learning Expectations

Through the meaningful context of creative writing, students will:

✓ Interpret a variety of illustrations, using evidence from the images and their own knowledge and experience

✓ Develop ability in creative, independent thinking, and ordering of ideas in a logical manner

✓ Communicate their ideas clearly and effectively

✓ Communicate their ideas for specific purposes and to specific audiences

✓ Apply previously learned basic skills of grammar, spelling, punctuation, and conventions of style and form

✓ Practice proofreading and editing skills

Table of Contents

Introduction

Cartoon Story Starters

This collection of 75 cartoons by an award-winning professional will inspire students' creative writing while making them laugh. Images of varying complexity are included so that students with a wide range of critical thinking and writing abilities may be engaged meaningfully. The illustrations may be used as "starters" for a variety of forms of writing, and can be used to augment any writing program. Or, use them as a meaningful "filler" activity when students have extra classroom time.

Organization of the Book

This resource is divided into five sections based on the primary genre of the illustrations:

1. Adventure
2. Careers
3. Fantasy
4. General Fiction
5. Sports

Each story starter worksheet includes an illustration and blank word box, a blank line for the story's title, and numbered blank lines for the story itself.

For easy reference, the story genre and illustration number are listed at the top of each page. Care has been taken to provide gender and racial balance.

The word box provides space for students to brainstorm key words.

Students should complete this list before writing to stimulate their creative thinking. The blank lines are numbered so that you may easily give students instructions on how long their creative writing piece should be.

Students may be given the Editing Checklist and Proofreader's Marks (page 5) either before or after writing a story. The checklist is a useful guide for proofreading their stories, and the chart of proofreader's marks lists the commonly used symbols, or shorthand, and their meanings.

How to Use the Illustrations

The cartoon story starters may be used as springboards for a variety of forms of creative writing. The most straightforward use is for a short story. Students who would benefit from other writing challenges may enjoy using the story starters to write any of the following:

- Poetry
- Biography or autobiography of a character in the illustration
- A letter written to or from a character
- Newspaper article or editorial about the event or issue represented in the illustration
- Diary or personal journal entry of a character
- Script for a play or movie
- And many other forms of writing!

The illustrations may also be used as a basis for dramatic presentations.

Name:_____

Story Title: _____

Editing Checklist

Put a checkmark next to the item once you have checked your writing and are satisfied that it is true.

◯   All verbs are in the same tense, either past or present.

◯   Each sentence begins with a capital letter and ends with the proper punctuation (period, question mark, or exclamation mark).

◯   Direct speech of characters begins and ends with quotations marks. (Example: "Hello," she said.)

◯   Apostrophes are used in the correct position in words to indicate possession. (Examples: the boy's bike, the boys' bikes)

◯   All words are spelled correctly.

◯   All sentences are complete.

◯   There are no run-on sentences.

◯   The first sentence of each new paragraph is indented.

Proofreader's Marks

Mark	Meaning	Mark	Meaning
⊙	Add a period	#	Put in a space
⋏	Add a comma	≡	Change to a capital letter
∧	Add a word or letter	/	Change to a lower case letter
⌄	Add an apostrophe		
＂ ＂	Add quotation marks	¶	Begin a new paragraph
ℓ	Remove	⸃	Indent the line (to begin a new paragraph)
⌣	Take out the space	sp	Spelling error

Word List

_____

_____

_____

_____

_____

_____

_____

Title: _____

1 _____

2 _____

3 _____

4 _____

5 _____

6 _____

7 _____

8 _____

9 _____

10 _____

11 _____

12 _____

13 _____

14 _____

15 _____

Name:_____

Word List

_____

_____

_____

_____

_____

_____

_____

Title:_____

1 _____

2 _____

3 _____

4 _____

5 _____

6 _____

7 _____

8 _____

9 _____

10 _____

11 _____

12 _____

13 _____

14 _____

15 _____

Name:_____

Word List

_____
_____
_____
_____
_____
_____
_____

Title:_____

1 _____
2 _____
3 _____
4 _____
5 _____
6 _____
7 _____
8 _____
9 _____
10 _____
11 _____
12 _____
13 _____
14 _____
15 _____

Name:_____

Word List

_____
_____
_____
_____
_____
_____
_____

Title:_____

1 _____

2 _____

3 _____

4 _____

5 _____

6 _____

7 _____

8 _____

9 _____

10 _____

11 _____

12 _____

13 _____

14 _____

15 _____

Name: _____

Word List

_____
_____
_____
_____
_____
_____
_____

Title: _____

1 _____
2 _____
3 _____
4 _____
5 _____
6 _____
7 _____
8 _____
9 _____
10 _____
11 _____
12 _____
13 _____
14 _____
15 _____

Name: _____

Word List

_____

_____

_____

_____

_____

_____

_____

Title: _____

1 _____

2 _____

3 _____

4 _____

5 _____

6 _____

7 _____

8 _____

9 _____

10 _____

11 _____

12 _____

13 _____

14 _____

15 _____

Name:_____

Word List

_____
_____
_____
_____
_____
_____
_____
_____

Title:_____

1 _____
2 _____
3 _____
4 _____
5 _____
6 _____
7 _____
8 _____
9 _____
10 _____
11 _____
12 _____
13 _____
14 _____
15 _____

Name: _____

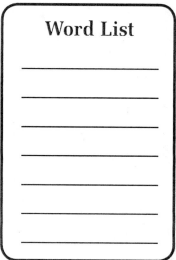

Word List

_____
_____
_____
_____
_____
_____
_____

Title: _____

1 _____
2 _____
3 _____
4 _____
5 _____
6 _____
7 _____
8 _____
9 _____
10 _____
11 _____
12 _____
13 _____
14 _____
15 _____

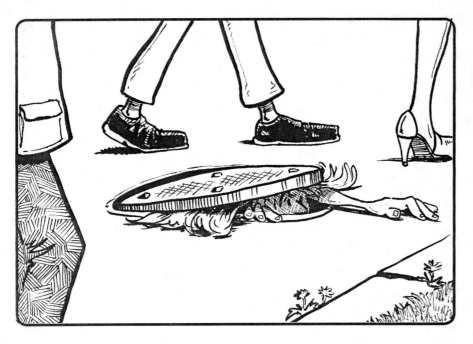

Word List

_____
_____
_____
_____
_____
_____
_____

Title:_____

1 _____
2 _____
3 _____
4 _____
5 _____
6 _____
7 _____
8 _____
9 _____
10 _____
11 _____
12 _____
13 _____
14 _____
15 _____

Name: _____

Word List

_____

_____

_____

_____

_____

_____

_____

Title: _____

1 _____

2 _____

3 _____

4 _____

5 _____

6 _____

7 _____

8 _____

9 _____

10 _____

11 _____

12 _____

13 _____

14 _____

15 _____

Name: _____

Word List

_____

_____

_____

_____

_____

_____

_____

Title: _____

1 _____

2 _____

3 _____

4 _____

5 _____

6 _____

7 _____

8 _____

9 _____

10 _____

11 _____

12 _____

13 _____

14 _____

15 _____

Name:_____

Word List

_____

_____

_____

_____

_____

_____

_____

Title:_____

1 _____

2 _____

3 _____

4 _____

5 _____

6 _____

7 _____

8 _____

9 _____

10 _____

11 _____

12 _____

13 _____

14 _____

15 _____

Name: _____

Word List

_____

_____

_____

_____

_____

_____

Title: _____

1 _____

2 _____

3 _____

4 _____

5 _____

6 _____

7 _____

8 _____

9 _____

10 _____

11 _____

12 _____

13 _____

14 _____

15 _____

Word List

_____

_____

_____

_____

_____

_____

_____

Title: _____

1 _____

2 _____

3 _____

4 _____

5 _____

6 _____

7 _____

8 _____

9 _____

10 _____

11 _____

12 _____

13 _____

14 _____

15 _____

Name: _____

Word List

_____

_____

_____

_____

_____

_____

_____

Title: _____

1 _____

2 _____

3 _____

4 _____

5 _____

6 _____

7 _____

8 _____

9 _____

10 _____

11 _____

12 _____

13 _____

14 _____

15 _____

Name:_____

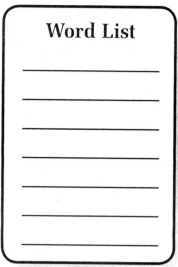

Word List

_____

_____

_____

_____

_____

_____

_____

Title: _____

1 _____

2 _____

3 _____

4 _____

5 _____

6 _____

7 _____

8 _____

9 _____

10 _____

11 _____

12 _____

13 _____

14 _____

15 _____

Word List

_____
_____
_____
_____
_____
_____
_____

Title: _____

1 _____
2 _____
3 _____
4 _____
5 _____
6 _____
7 _____
8 _____
9 _____
10 _____
11 _____
12 _____
13 _____
14 _____
15 _____

Name:_____

Word List

_____
_____
_____
_____
_____
_____
_____

Title:_____

1 _____
2 _____
3 _____
4 _____
5 _____
6 _____
7 _____
8 _____
9 _____
10 _____
11 _____
12 _____
13 _____
14 _____
15 _____

Name: _____

Word List

_____

_____

_____

_____

_____

_____

_____

Title: _____

1 _____

2 _____

3 _____

4 _____

5 _____

6 _____

7 _____

8 _____

9 _____

10 _____

11 _____

12 _____

13 _____

14 _____

15 _____

Word List

_____

_____

_____

_____

_____

_____

_____

Title: _____

1 _____

2 _____

3 _____

4 _____

5 _____

6 _____

7 _____

8 _____

9 _____

10 _____

11 _____

12 _____

13 _____

14 _____

15 _____

Name:_____

Word List

_____

_____

_____

_____

_____

_____

Title:_____

1 _____

2 _____

3 _____

4 _____

5 _____

6 _____

7 _____

8 _____

9 _____

10 _____

11 _____

12 _____

13 _____

14 _____

15 _____

Name: _____

Word List

_____

_____

_____

_____

_____

_____

_____

Title: _____

1 _____

2 _____

3 _____

4 _____

5 _____

6 _____

7 _____

8 _____

9 _____

10 _____

11 _____

12 _____

13 _____

14 _____

15 _____

Name: _____

Word List

_____
_____
_____
_____
_____
_____
_____

Title: _____

1 _____
2 _____
3 _____
4 _____
5 _____
6 _____
7 _____
8 _____
9 _____
10 _____
11 _____
12 _____
13 _____
14 _____
15 _____

Title:_____

1 _____
2 _____
3 _____
4 _____
5 _____
6 _____
7 _____
8 _____
9 _____
10 _____
11 _____
12 _____
13 _____
14 _____
15 _____

Name: _____

Word List

_____

_____

_____

_____

_____

_____

_____

Title: _____

1 _____

2 _____

3 _____

4 _____

5 _____

6 _____

7 _____

8 _____

9 _____

10 _____

11 _____

12 _____

13 _____

14 _____

15 _____

Name:_____

Word List

_____

_____

_____

_____

_____

_____

_____

Title:_____

1 _____

2 _____

3 _____

4 _____

5 _____

6 _____

7 _____

8 _____

9 _____

10 _____

11 _____

12 _____

13 _____

14 _____

15 _____

Name: _____

Word List

_____
_____
_____
_____
_____
_____
_____

Title: _____

1 _____
2 _____
3 _____
4 _____
5 _____
6 _____
7 _____
8 _____
9 _____
10 _____
11 _____
12 _____
13 _____
14 _____
15 _____

Name: _____

Word List

_____
_____
_____
_____
_____
_____
_____

Title: _____

1 _____
2 _____
3 _____
4 _____
5 _____
6 _____
7 _____
8 _____
9 _____
10 _____
11 _____
12 _____
13 _____
14 _____
15 _____

Name: _____

Word List

_____
_____
_____
_____
_____
_____

Title: _____

1 _____
2 _____
3 _____
4 _____
5 _____
6 _____
7 _____
8 _____
9 _____
10 _____
11 _____
12 _____
13 _____
14 _____
15 _____

Name:_____

Word List

_____

_____

_____

_____

_____

_____

_____

Title: _____

1 _____

2 _____

3 _____

4 _____

5 _____

6 _____

7 _____

8 _____

9 _____

10 _____

11 _____

12 _____

13 _____

14 _____

15 _____

Word List

_____
_____
_____
_____
_____
_____
_____

Title: _____

1 _____
2 _____
3 _____
4 _____
5 _____
6 _____
7 _____
8 _____
9 _____
10 _____
11 _____
12 _____
13 _____
14 _____
15 _____

Name: _____

Word List

_____
_____
_____
_____
_____
_____
_____

Title: _____

1 _____
2 _____
3 _____
4 _____
5 _____
6 _____
7 _____
8 _____
9 _____
10 _____
11 _____
12 _____
13 _____
14 _____
15 _____

Word List

_____

_____

_____

_____

_____

_____

_____

Title: _____

1 _____

2 _____

3 _____

4 _____

5 _____

6 _____

7 _____

8 _____

9 _____

10 _____

11 _____

12 _____

13 _____

14 _____

15 _____

Name:_____

Word List

_____

_____

_____

_____

_____

_____

_____

Title:_____

1 _____

2 _____

3 _____

4 _____

5 _____

6 _____

7 _____

8 _____

9 _____

10 _____

11 _____

12 _____

13 _____

14 _____

15 _____

Word List

_____
_____
_____
_____
_____
_____
_____

Title: _____

1 _____
2 _____
3 _____
4 _____
5 _____
6 _____
7 _____
8 _____
9 _____
10 _____
11 _____
12 _____
13 _____
14 _____
15 _____

Name: _____

Word List

_____
_____
_____
_____
_____
_____
_____

Title: _____

1 _____
2 _____
3 _____
4 _____
5 _____
6 _____
7 _____
8 _____
9 _____
10 _____
11 _____
12 _____
13 _____
14 _____
15 _____

Word List

_____

_____

_____

_____

_____

_____

_____

Title:_____

1 _____

2 _____

3 _____

4 _____

5 _____

6 _____

7 _____

8 _____

9 _____

10 _____

11 _____

12 _____

13 _____

14 _____

15 _____

Name:_____

Word List

_____
_____
_____
_____
_____
_____
_____

Title: _____

1 _____

2 _____

3 _____

4 _____

5 _____

6 _____

7 _____

8 _____

9 _____

10 _____

11 _____

12 _____

13 _____

14 _____

15 _____

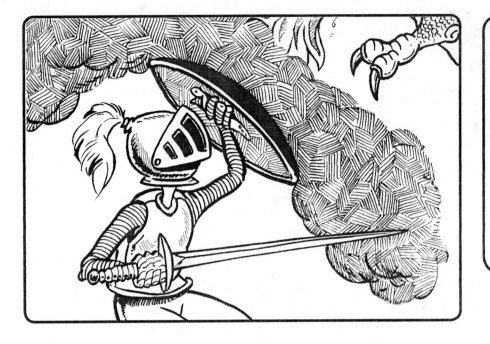

Word List

_____
_____
_____
_____
_____
_____
_____

Title: _____

1 _____
2 _____
3 _____
4 _____
5 _____
6 _____
7 _____
8 _____
9 _____
10 _____
11 _____
12 _____
13 _____
14 _____
15 _____

Name: _____

Word List

_____

_____

_____

_____

_____

_____

_____

Title: _____

1 _____

2 _____

3 _____

4 _____

5 _____

6 _____

7 _____

8 _____

9 _____

10 _____

11 _____

12 _____

13 _____

14 _____

15 _____

Name: _____

Word List

_____
_____
_____
_____
_____
_____
_____

Title: _____

1 _____
2 _____
3 _____
4 _____
5 _____
6 _____
7 _____
8 _____
9 _____
10 _____
11 _____
12 _____
13 _____
14 _____
15 _____

Name: _____

Word List

_____

_____

_____

_____

_____

_____

_____

Title: _____

1 _____

2 _____

3 _____

4 _____

5 _____

6 _____

7 _____

8 _____

9 _____

10 _____

11 _____

12 _____

13 _____

14 _____

15 _____

Word List

_____

_____

_____

_____

_____

_____

_____

Title: _____

1 _____

2 _____

3 _____

4 _____

5 _____

6 _____

7 _____

8 _____

9 _____

10 _____

11 _____

12 _____

13 _____

14 _____

15 _____

Word List

_____
_____
_____
_____
_____
_____
_____

Title: _____

1 _____
2 _____
3 _____
4 _____
5 _____
6 _____
7 _____
8 _____
9 _____
10 _____
11 _____
12 _____
13 _____
14 _____
15 _____

Title: _____

1 _____

2 _____

3 _____

4 _____

5 _____

6 _____

7 _____

8 _____

9 _____

10 _____

11 _____

12 _____

13 _____

14 _____

15 _____

Name:_____

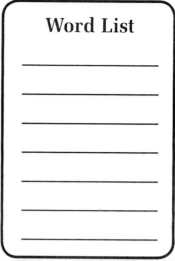

Word List

_____

_____

_____

_____

_____

_____

_____

Title: _____

1 _____

2 _____

3 _____

4 _____

5 _____

6 _____

7 _____

8 _____

9 _____

10 _____

11 _____

12 _____

13 _____

14 _____

15 _____

Title:_____

1 _____

2 _____

3 _____

4 _____

5 _____

6 _____

7 _____

8 _____

9 _____

10 _____

11 _____

12 _____

13 _____

14 _____

15 _____

Word List

_____
_____
_____
_____
_____
_____
_____

Title: _____

1 _____
2 _____
3 _____
4 _____
5 _____
6 _____
7 _____
8 _____
9 _____
10 _____
11 _____
12 _____
13 _____
14 _____
15 _____

Word List

_____

_____

_____

_____

_____

_____

_____

Title: _____

1 _____

2 _____

3 _____

4 _____

5 _____

6 _____

7 _____

8 _____

9 _____

10 _____

11 _____

12 _____

13 _____

14 _____

15 _____

Word List

_____

_____

_____

_____

_____

_____

_____

Title: _____

1 _____

2 _____

3 _____

4 _____

5 _____

6 _____

7 _____

8 _____

9 _____

10 _____

11 _____

12 _____

13 _____

14 _____

15 _____

Name:_____

Word List

_____
_____
_____
_____
_____
_____
_____

Title:_____

1 _____
2 _____
3 _____
4 _____
5 _____
6 _____
7 _____
8 _____
9 _____
10 _____
11 _____
12 _____
13 _____
14 _____
15 _____

Name:_____

Title: _____

1 _____

2 _____

3 _____

4 _____

5 _____

6 _____

7 _____

8 _____

9 _____

10 _____

11 _____

12 _____

13 _____

14 _____

15 _____

Word List

_____
_____
_____
_____
_____
_____
_____

Title: _____

1 _____
2 _____
3 _____
4 _____
5 _____
6 _____
7 _____
8 _____
9 _____
10 _____
11 _____
12 _____
13 _____
14 _____
15 _____

Name: _____

Word List

_____
_____
_____
_____
_____
_____
_____

Title: _____

1 _____
2 _____
3 _____
4 _____
5 _____
6 _____
7 _____
8 _____
9 _____
10 _____
11 _____
12 _____
13 _____
14 _____
15 _____

Name:_____

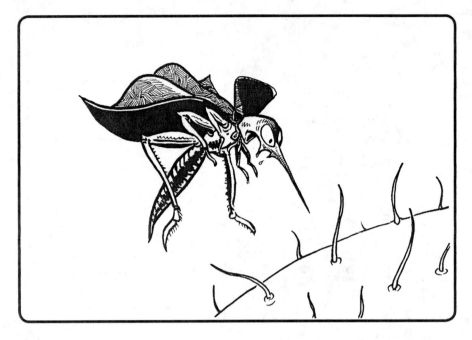

Word List

_____

_____

_____

_____

_____

_____

_____

Title: _____

1 _____

2 _____

3 _____

4 _____

5 _____

6 _____

7 _____

8 _____

9 _____

10 _____

11 _____

12 _____

13 _____

14 _____

15 _____

Name:_____

Word List

_____
_____
_____
_____
_____
_____
_____

Title:_____

1 _____
2 _____
3 _____
4 _____
5 _____
6 _____
7 _____
8 _____
9 _____
10 _____
11 _____
12 _____
13 _____
14 _____
15 _____

Name: _____

Word List

_____
_____
_____
_____
_____
_____
_____

Title: _____

1 _____
2 _____
3 _____
4 _____
5 _____
6 _____
7 _____
8 _____
9 _____
10 _____
11 _____
12 _____
13 _____
14 _____
15 _____

Name: _____

Word List

_____

_____

_____

_____

_____

_____

_____

Title: _____

1 _____

2 _____

3 _____

4 _____

5 _____

6 _____

7 _____

8 _____

9 _____

10 _____

11 _____

12 _____

13 _____

14 _____

15 _____

Name: _____

Word List

_____

_____

_____

_____

_____

_____

_____

Title: _____

1 _____

2 _____

3 _____

4 _____

5 _____

6 _____

7 _____

8 _____

9 _____

10 _____

11 _____

12 _____

13 _____

14 _____

15 _____

Word List

_____

_____

_____

_____

_____

_____

_____

Title: _____

1 _____

2 _____

3 _____

4 _____

5 _____

6 _____

7 _____

8 _____

9 _____

10 _____

11 _____

12 _____

13 _____

14 _____

15 _____

Name: _____

Word List

_____
_____
_____
_____
_____
_____

Title: _____

1 _____
2 _____
3 _____
4 _____
5 _____
6 _____
7 _____
8 _____
9 _____
10 _____
11 _____
12 _____
13 _____
14 _____
15 _____

Word List

_____

_____

_____

_____

_____

_____

_____

Title: _____

1 _____

2 _____

3 _____

4 _____

5 _____

6 _____

7 _____

8 _____

9 _____

10 _____

11 _____

12 _____

13 _____

14 _____

15 _____

Name: _____

Word List

_____

_____

_____

_____

_____

_____

_____

Title: _____

1 _____

2 _____

3 _____

4 _____

5 _____

6 _____

7 _____

8 _____

9 _____

10 _____

11 _____

12 _____

13 _____

14 _____

15 _____

Name:_____

Word List

_____
_____
_____
_____
_____
_____
_____

Title: _____

1 _____
2 _____
3 _____
4 _____
5 _____
6 _____
7 _____
8 _____
9 _____
10 _____
11 _____
12 _____
13 _____
14 _____
15 _____

Word List

_____
_____
_____
_____
_____
_____
_____

Title: _____

1 _____
2 _____
3 _____
4 _____
5 _____
6 _____
7 _____
8 _____
9 _____
10 _____
11 _____
12 _____
13 _____
14 _____
15 _____

Name: _____

Word List

_____

_____

_____

_____

_____

_____

_____

Title: _____

1 _____

2 _____

3 _____

4 _____

5 _____

6 _____

7 _____

8 _____

9 _____

10 _____

11 _____

12 _____

13 _____

14 _____

15 _____

Word List

_____

_____

_____

_____

_____

_____

_____

Title:_____

1 _____
2 _____
3 _____
4 _____
5 _____
6 _____
7 _____
8 _____
9 _____
10 _____
11 _____
12 _____
13 _____
14 _____
15 _____

Name:_____

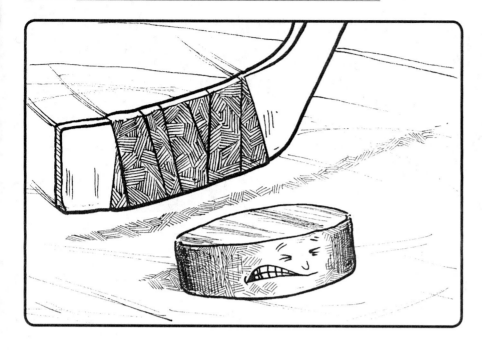

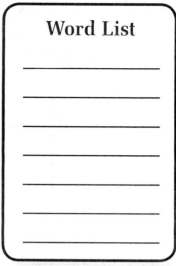

Word List

_____
_____
_____
_____
_____
_____
_____

Title:_____

1 _____
2 _____
3 _____
4 _____
5 _____
6 _____
7 _____
8 _____
9 _____
10 _____
11 _____
12 _____
13 _____
14 _____
15 _____

Name:_____

Word List

_____

_____

_____

_____

_____

_____

_____

Title:_____

1 _____

2 _____

3 _____

4 _____

5 _____

6 _____

7 _____

8 _____

9 _____

10 _____

11 _____

12 _____

13 _____

14 _____

15 _____

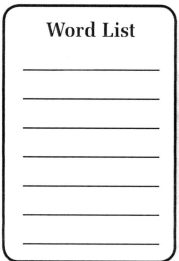

Word List

_____

_____

_____

_____

_____

_____

_____

Title: _____

1 _____

2 _____

3 _____

4 _____

5 _____

6 _____

7 _____

8 _____

9 _____

10 _____

11 _____

12 _____

13 _____

14 _____

15 _____

Word List

_____

_____

_____

_____

_____

_____

Title: _____

1 _____

2 _____

3 _____

4 _____

5 _____

6 _____

7 _____

8 _____

9 _____

10 _____

11 _____

12 _____

13 _____

14 _____

15 _____

Name:_____

Word List

_____

_____

_____

_____

_____

_____

_____

Title:_____

1 _____

2 _____

3 _____

4 _____

5 _____

6 _____

7 _____

8 _____

9 _____

10 _____

11 _____

12 _____

13 _____

14 _____

15 _____

Name: _____

Title: _____

1 _____

2 _____

3 _____

4 _____

5 _____

6 _____

7 _____

8 _____

9 _____

10 _____

11 _____

12 _____

13 _____

14 _____

15 _____

Word List

_____
_____
_____
_____
_____
_____
_____

Title: _____

1 _____
2 _____
3 _____
4 _____
5 _____
6 _____
7 _____
8 _____
9 _____
10 _____
11 _____
12 _____
13 _____
14 _____
15 _____

Word List

_____

_____

_____

_____

_____

_____

_____

Title: _____

1 _____

2 _____

3 _____

4 _____

5 _____

6 _____

7 _____

8 _____

9 _____

10 _____

11 _____

12 _____

13 _____

14 _____

15 _____